I'm Judgmental, You're Judgmental

Also by the author from Paulist Press—

Accepting the Troll Underneath the Bridge

I'M JUDGMENTAL, YOU'RE JUDGMENTAL

Healing Our Condemning Attitudes

Terry D. Cooper

Paulist Press
New York/Mahwah, New Jersey

Cover design and interior illustrations by Nicholas T. Markell.

Library of Congress Cataloging-in-Publication Data

Cooper, Terry D.
    I'm judgmental, you're judgmental : healing our condemning attitudes / Terry D. Cooper.
        p.   cm.
    ISBN 0-8091-3870-0 (alk. paper)
    1. Judgment—Religious aspects—Christianity.   2. Authoritarianism (Personality trait)—Religious aspects—Christianity. I. Title.
BV4597.54.C66   1999
248.4—dc21   99-14353
                                                                   CIP

Published by Paulist Press
997 Macarthur Boulevard
Mahwah, New Jersey 07430

www.paulistpress.com

Printed and bound in the
United States of America

Contents

I wish to acknowledge Dr. Robert L. Asa's contribution to chapter three's distinctions between making healthy judgments and being judgmental. Thanks, Bob.

This book is dedicated, with love and gratitude, to my parents, Don and Barbara Cooper.

Introduction

For quite some time, I have wanted to write a book about "judgmentalism," as long as it dealt with *other* people. I've been quick to spot in people rigid, authoritarian attitudes and statements that I did not like very much. I especially reacted when I perceived this narrow-minded mentality in the world of religion. A critical, shaming, condescending demeanor was bad enough, but to claim it in the name of religion—that was too much. So I began to throw stones at the judgmental stone-throwers. The black and white, simplistic reduction of complex issues seemed inhumane and unsatisfactory. How proud I was to point this out!

I engaged in a reactionary protest against judgmental thinking. I attacked all the stereotyping, labeling, pigeonholing, and smug sense of absolute certainty that went along with a rigid mentality. What I did not realize, of course, is that I was what family systems theorist Murray Bowen frequently calls "negatively fused" to judgmentalism. By constantly reacting to it, it was controlling me. I *had* to fight it. Like a child stuck in defiance, I associated freedom with perpetual rebellion.

What I also did not realize is that my harsh condemnation of judgmental people was every bit as judgmental as anything *they* were doing. I was becoming a narrow-minded defender of open-mindedness. I was intolerant of intolerance. I was a zealous missionary who grandiosely thought it was my job to expand people's thinking. I was going to "control" those awful controlling tendencies in other people. While the content of what I was saying may have differed from the judgmental attitudes I had encountered, the process of my thinking was the same.

I began to realize that judgmentalism and authoritarian thinking can come in many clothes. Again, I had recognized it only in perspectives I didn't like. Now I must put my own style or manner of thinking under a microscope. I began to realize that a judgmental mentality can pop up in practically every area of life. In fact, many of us who pride ourselves on having transcended the narrow confines of rigid thinking are actually stuck in thought patterns that are very inflexible. I, myself, have often been most self-righteous in pointing out the self-righteousness of others.

My point is simply this: When we think we have completely eliminated judgmentalism from our thinking, we probably need to take another look. Judgmental, authoritarian thinking is insidious, often sliding into our thoughts during times of anxiety and insecurity. It is not just "the other person's problem." In fact, it is *everyone's* predicament. We can certainly make steps toward recognizing and changing it within ourselves, yet we will most likely never be completely free of it.

This brings us to a very important realization: The world is not simply divided between judgmental and nonjudgmental people. Everyone is judgmental in some ways and nonjudgmental in others. This is not an either/or issue. Therefore, we need to approach this topic with humility, compassion, and an awareness that unwarranted pride may have entered our own way of thinking.

Judgmental people (a category that at one time or

another includes all of us) need our love, not our judgments. Sometimes they are very hard people to love. Yet if we extend to them the very judgments we so often receive from them, we perpetuate a cycle of intolerance that can lead to hatred.

It is doubtful that any of us *really believe* we are closed-minded. We want to see ourselves as being fair. It is important, therefore, to be able to drop our guard long enough to examine carefully our own dispositions. Many times, however, our anger and protest against other viewpoints cloud our rationality and we pontificate from our emotional reactions. While we may strain to be cordial, our private conversations include all-or-nothing expletives to describe a "stupid" idea or "crazy" person. Even in colleges and universities, where flexible thinking and open-mindedness are presented as ideals, there is often a stubborn resistance and dogmatic campaign against other perspectives. Lip-service may be given to a respect for diversity, but there are often tremendous infighting and "put-downs" of people with alternative beliefs. At times, it is very difficult to find a balance in discussions where a variety of opinions are represented.

The Disadvantages of "Open-mindedness"

While open-minded people may have an understanding of several viewpoints, the mere fact that they know so many views exist may make them hesitant, careful, and even timid. We are, after all, normally less prone toward zealous claims when we notice the massive array of angles available. In other words, the more we fairly examine alternative positions, the more inclined we may be to doubt ourselves.

In many conversations, it is easy to detect "second-

3

guessers" from "non-second-guessers." Second-guessers are filled with thoughts such as "There may be something else to see," "Perhaps others see something I don't," or "Maybe my viewpoint is limited." Conversely, non-second-guessers march ahead like cognitive bulls, often with a display of self-assurance. They *know* who's right! Convictions are set in stone. Their passionate argument need not be "bothered" with the cumbersome task of listening to alternatives. Their minds are made up!

The authoritative mannerisms of the "non-second-guessers" often provoke even more self-doubt and insecurity in the "second-guesser." After all, things seem to be so obvious to their partners in dialogue. If things appear that evident, maybe the second-guesser should listen again. After all, they may be wrong.

A nonquestioning mentality or "cognitive style" creates enormous problems in marriage. "Non-second-guessers" are macho thinkers (though they may be male *or* female). Being "sure" often involves being dominant. Hesitation is perceived as weakness; confusion is seen as immature; "bottom lines" are easy to detect; ethical issues are clear-cut; other cultures are strange; gender differences are clearly defined; and intelligence is associated with fast thinking.

The problems between a "second guesser" and a "non-second-guesser" are easily illustrated in the marriage of Gail and Ed. Gail knows that her own ideas are somewhat limited and so she values the perspectives of others. She believes we all have "blinders" and may not see ourselves as we actually are. Most of the time, she enters a discussion with this awareness. A certain amount of self-doubt, she thinks, is part of a healthy personality that recognizes its own limits. This is a strength in Gail, *if* she gets together with another "second-guesser."

Gail's husband, Ed, however, is not a second-guesser. He has a bulldog certainty about anything he says. He can also be a tricky manipulator of reality. Clinging to his viewpoint *no matter what,* Ed maneuvers Gail into taking far more responsibility for the marriage than she needs to take. He has endless defenses that excuse his own responsibility and point a finger back at Gail. A smooth and seemingly certain person, Ed comes across so well that he naturally sends Gail into a tailspin of self-doubt. While Gail has an ability that Ed actually needs (the capacity to doubt himself), Gail is always at a disadvantage as she tries to be fair with Ed's relentless certainty. Gail, an educated, healthy adult, nearly lets the non-second-guessing tactics of Ed make her crazy.

Another disadvantage to open-minded thinking is the loss of colorful expletives and inflammatory language. Judgmental language is powerful language. It makes us feel strong when we use it. It is, after all, the vehicle of shame. It is also deceptive in that it makes us believe we are as certain as we sound.

Fair, nonjudgmental language is less interesting. It tends to be calm, sober, and careful about the words it chooses. It forces us to use our minds and not simply rely upon strong emotion. It doesn't pulverize anyone. It does not draw a lot of "oohs" and "ahs" from an audience. Nonjudgmental language will not rely on inflammatory soundbites, regardless of how much attention that might attract.

A sad fact is that our public discourse often revolves around irrational exaggeration and hype. In order to make a point, we often grossly overstate it. In any campaign year, for instance, just listen to the bombastic words and grandiose zeal of many politicians. The careful, respecting attitude that sees some legitimacy in another's opposing viewpoint is completely lost. It's a rigid, mudslinging world of easy right-and-wrong answers. Being accurate is far less important than being colorful.

"Soundbites," those quick, fiery expressions that squeeze complex issues into trite cliches, are unfortunately appealing to many. This is the world of easy pronouncements and generalizations. These bumper-sticker phrases help many come across very well on televised talk shows and media events. A person who makes a sincere attempt to address all sides of the issue is either cut off or brushed aside as wishy-washy and lacking in convictions. We don't have time to hear that person out. The person who speaks in simplistic, black-or-white language and who doesn't do justice to the complexity of the question often fares the best.

Judgmental thinking is also not burdened with the task of empathy. Perhaps the central feature of judgmental thinking is that it always lacks empathy. As Carl Rogers, a founder of humanistic psychology, pointed out so well, empathy is that capacity to enter another's viewpoint and understand life from that angle. It is primarily a cognitive exercise. While it involves understanding someone's feelings, it is essentially a mental process of deep, nonjudgmental listening in which we risk taking on another person's perspective. Rogers discusses this kind of listening with a client.

> To sense the client's inner world of private personal meanings as if it were your own, but without ever losing the "as if" quality, this is empathy, and this seems essential to a growth-promoting relationship. To sense his confusion or his timidity or his anger or his feeling of being treated unfairly as if it were your own, yet

without your own uncertainty or fear or anger or suspicion getting bound up in it, this is the condition I am endeavoring to describe....It is this kind of highly personal empathy which seems important in making it possible for a person to get close to himself and to learn, to change and develop....I suspect that each of us has discovered that this kind of understanding is extremely rare. We neither receive it nor offer it with any great frequency. Instead we offer another type of understanding which is very different, such as "I understand what is wrong with you" or "I understand what makes you act that way." These are the types of understanding which we usually offer and receive—an evaluative understanding from the outside. It is not surprising that we shy away from true understanding. If I am truly open to the way life is experienced by another person—if I can take his world into mine—then I run the risk of seeing life in his way, of being changed myself, and we all resist change. So we tend to view this other person's world only in our own terms, not in his. We analyze and evaluate it. We do not understand it. But when someone understands how it feels and seems to be me, without wanting to analyze or judge me, then I can blossom and grow in that climate. I am sure I am not alone in that feeling....None of us steadily achieves such a complete empathy as I have been trying to describe, any more than we can achieve complete congruence, but there is no doubt that individuals can develop along this line.[1]

Empathy does *not* mean approving of all aspects of another's beliefs or behavior. It does, however, necessitate giving the perspective "air time," and listening with new ears and less preconceived ideas. Again, as Rogers has pointed out so well, there are profound risks in developing a lifestyle of empathic listening. We may completely change our minds, or at least be significantly moved by another person's perspective. We may walk away from the conversation with far less certainty than we had before. Whatever the results, however, we will feel the fulfillment of having respected the person underneath the viewpoint.

Viktor Frankl, survivor of a concentration camp and the founder of logotherapy, also points to the extreme importance of affirming another's dignity through empathic listening. He relates the following experience with one of his patients.

> Recently, I received a telephone call at three in the morning from a lady who told me that she was determined to commit suicide but was curious to know what I would say about it. I replied with all the arguments against this resolution and for survival, and I talked to her for thirty minutes—until she finally gave her word that she would not take her life but rather come to see me in the hospital. But when she visited there it turned out that not one of all the arguments I offered had impressed her. The only reason she had decided not to commit suicide was the fact that, rather than growing angry because of having been disturbed in my sleep in the middle of the night, I had patiently listened to her and talked with her for half an hour, and a world—she found—in which this can happen, must be a world worth living in.[2]

While nonjudgmental thinking may not be the easiest way to relate to others, it is certainly the way of Jesus. Jesus constantly addresses us as more than our past, seeing the possibility of newness no matter how debilitating our backgrounds. He calls us out of where we have been and into who we are—loved, accepted, and unconditionally valued. A self-destructive life is lived outside the Good News that we don't have to fight, run away from, or deny our inner condemnations. God embraces us *through* them. This nonjudgmental attitude is what makes us able to hear and follow the voice of grace. Jesus meets us precisely where we are and simply says, "Follow me." He does *not* say, "I condemn you. Go clean up your life and *then* you can follow me." He knows that his acceptance will provide the desire and motivation within us for change. His message is, "Trust the future, for it is in God's hands. Don't let today's anxieties stir within you a desire to judge yourself or others. That's beyond your limits, anyway. Don't let judgment close you off from a new world of adventure. When the frowning curtain of judgment is pulled back, you can catch a glimpse of a God who smiles."

CHAPTER ONE

Understanding Judgmental
Thinking

So what does judgmental thinking "look like"? Can we recognize it within ourselves? Does it have common, identifiable features? If so, what are they? Here are some primary attributes.

J ustifies ourselves, in spite of our faults
U nderstands only its own viewpoint
D enounces persons, rather than behavior or ideas
G randiose thinking disconnects from humility
M akes us more and more alienated from our "dark side"
E nhances self-righteousness through putting down others
N eeds other people's "sins" in order to dodge oneself
T urns away from grace and acceptance of self and others
A voids the anxiety of seeing life's complexities
L oves "labels" as a form of security

Let's look, in more detail, at each one of these characteristics.

Justifies ourselves, in spite of our faults. A judgmental attitude serves a very important function: it keeps our attention away from our own faults and focused on the shortcomings of others. Much of judgmentalism can be understood in terms of a cyclical process: neglecting, projecting, and protecting. Here's how it works: At times in our lives we lose focus on ourselves and what we need to do for self-care. We quit exploring our own shortcomings, quit sweeping our own doorstep, stop looking at areas in our lives that need work. Self-inventory is lacking. Soon we begin to lose any sort of humility. It's a short step from not being aware of our shortcomings to saying we have none. Self-alienation emerges. We may find we carry a low-grade sense of annoyance and do not know why. Unconsciously, we may be starting to feel some self-disgust and confusion.

As we progressively become strangers to our own dark side, we may start "seeing" that image in others. In other words, we may very well push our own unacknowledged garbage onto others. They conveniently serve as targets for our own self-disgust and frustration. Our neglected problems are pushed outward as we indict anyone or anything external to us. We need others in order to continue to avoid ourselves. Without them, we'd have to look within.

Neglecting and projecting are a nifty way of protecting ourselves. It keeps the heat off us. We can feel superior and condescending as "their" disturbance, sickness, or sin serves as a marvelous distraction. We have insulation. Using other people's failings as a way of avoiding ourselves can almost become addictive. It provides relief, refuge, and is a wonderful distraction from ourselves. Other people's inadequacies become our hangout. The television preacher who must find a "sin" to rail against; the teacher who needs to talk about how indifferent and impossible students are; the alcoholic father who is obsessed with his son's possible "pot" problem; the pedophile who constantly protests pornography in his community; the psychiatrist who cynically talks about how selfishly neurotic his patients are. All of these people can easily become obsessed with their mechanism of self-avoidance. Other people's dilemmas and problems become their ticket out of looking carefully at themselves, their marriages, relationships, parenting abilities, and so on.

Understands only its own viewpoint. In a sense, judgmental thinking is intoxicated with its own perspective. When we are the most judgmental, we are not really able to think freely. It is not so much that we have rigid thoughts; instead, it is that rigid thoughts *have us!* We are prisoners of our thinking, unable to get outside, underneath, or beyond it enough to see with comprehension. We are unreachable, drunk on the wine of our own certainty.

This inability to take on other perspectives creates enormous limits in our relationships with others. Most of us have had the experience of trying to talk with someone who will not even try to see our angle on things. This, of course, can be enormously frustrating. The annoyance is not so much that the other person disagrees with us, but rather, that he or she won't even hear us in the first place. Our outlook is simply not given a chance. Such people believe that recognizing any legitimacy to our viewpoint automatically means giving up their own. Consequently, no value is seen in anything we are trying to say.

Perspective-taking abilities may well be one of the most important relationship skills we can ever develop. When we are completely absorbed by our own vision of things, we obviously cannot benefit from anybody else's angle.

Stubbornly clinging to only our own viewpoint may *seem* like a strength, but it is deceptive. We may simply say that we "have strong convictions" or that "we are not being wishy-washy." We may even call it "moral courage" when we are unable to hear another perspective. However, viewpoints that don't allow us to look at alternatives have little value.

Denounces persons, rather than behavior or ideas. Some acts of behavior definitely need to be judged. However, a judgmental mentality is never content to stop there. It is not just the behavior, but the entire person, who must be judged. A person arrested for shoplifting becomes "a no-good thief." A person who acts inconsistently with his or her children is "a lousy parent." A woman who goes through a period of promiscuity in her life is "a slut." Someone with strong opinions about the Bible is "just a religious fanatic." A soft-hearted, sentimental person is a "bleeding-heart liberal." A person out of work is a "bum." Someone interested in academics is an "egg head." An uniformed individual is an "idiot."

It is very easy to make a swift leap from criticizing someone's behavior to evaluating the entire person beneath the behavior. It is very tempting to equate the whole person with a singular, obnoxious behavior. Even when we know that this unfairly reduces a human being to a particular act, it is still very easy to do. It's an irrational leap to an unwarranted conclusion. And more importantly, it minimizes the complexity of human personality as it "defines" a person by a singular act. Yet, particularly when a behavior triggers a strong emotional reaction in us, we are normally quite eager to condemn everything about the person. Perhaps the best example of this is sexual abuse. Many of us may feel so outraged and angry at a perpetrator of child sexual abuse that we see the pedophile as merely a "pervert." All other aspects of the individual's personality fade. We are so appalled by the activity that we want to quickly condemn the man. Of course the man is responsible for this despicable action. Of course the man should be held accountable for this behavior. Of course what he did was wrong. Yet, his entire personality or being cannot be brushed away with the wave of a condemning hand. He is more than a sexual offender.

Grandiose thinking disconnects from humility. A common theme in judgmentalism is a loss of humility. This loss of humility goes beyond the passing thought that we are better than someone. It is based on pervasive attitudes and mental errors that deny our human limitations. Let's look at these.

First, judgmentalism does indeed involve a sense of moral superiority. This is one of the primary reasons that Jesus tells us in Matthew 7:1 to "Judge not." As we judge another person, we are acting as spectator, not as player. We are pushing aside our own shortcomings, faults, limits, and finitude while we assess another. But once we get off the bleachers and into the game, we may find that life is much more complex than our spectator position had realized.

Second, judgmentalism also involves a deep sense of intellectual superiority insofar as we believe we are capable of evaluating the entire context of another's life, with all its variables. It is an arrogant illusion that we can "size up" someone's entire life. We simply don't know the whole story. Perhaps one of the reasons Jesus warned so rigorously against judgmentalism is that it makes a "god" or "idol" of our own viewpoint. Judgmentalism always means forgetting our finitude. Somehow we've found a "place" on which to give a final estimate of another.

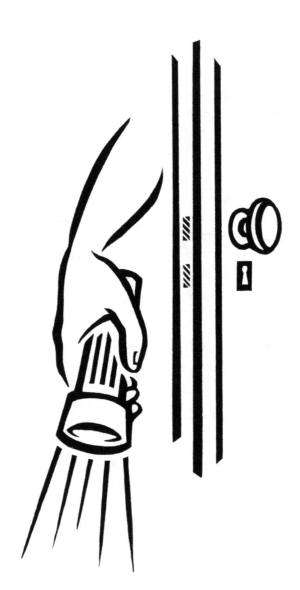

We don't know how someone has been hurt, the struggles of their life, the overall context out of which they have lived. Some may think this sounds dangerously close to "excusing" another's behavior, but this is not at all what I am suggesting. I am simply saying that we, coming out of our own set of assumptions, viewpoints, limitations, and cognitive finitude, cannot possibly deliver a "final verdict" about another's *entire* life. We may have very definite judgments about specific *acts* this person has committed. But we just don't have the intellectual resources to determine the nature of his or her entire existence.

Makes us more and more alienated from our "dark side." When we are shocked and preoccupied with the "horrible" actions of others, our attention is removed from our own destructive behavior. Focused on the deplorable behavior of outsiders, we are freed from looking at ourselves. In fact, we can tell ourselves that their behavior is "unthinkable" or "unimaginable." We could never do something like that!

Harsh condemnations of others indicate a lack of grace and tender acceptance in our own lives. With so many things being unacceptable, we are afraid to shine the flashlight into our own closets. Consequently, we remain ignorant of our own hidden motives, unconscious motivations, and capability of destructive behavior. We are simply afraid to explore ourselves. Why? Because we don't want those judgmental guns pointed at us. We don't have enough grace and acceptance to freely make that inward journey. The fear of condemnation is much greater than the assurance of acceptance.

Enhances self-righteousness through putting down others. One of the biggest psychological pay-offs of judgmentalism is feeling proud that we are not like "those other people." When we condemn others, we usually feel superior ourselves. We are "one-up" on them. Once again, we are not a participant in the game, but instead a sideline spectator and judge of the game. Temporarily forgetting our own humanity, we feel entitled to evaluate another human being. In fact, it's very easy to fall in love with the job of measuring and ranking others.

We may not consciously be aware of how much we inflate ourselves by tearing down others. Consciously, we may tell ourselves, "I wouldn't think of doing such a thing," "I could never do that," or "I am shocked and aghast at such behavior." We are usually noting how utterly different we are from these people, or how we would simply never sink to their level. Criticizing others is not just an offensive move against them; it is also a defensive move to protect our own purity.

For instance, I am generally quick to recognize when people are self-absorbed or self-centered. I can even feel a sense of disgust at such self-involvement. I can point out how oblivious they are to the needs of those around them. I can easily resent the manner in which they dominate conversations, think only of their own issues, and rarely place their focus on another. I can do all this so well because *I* am often in my own little world, self-preoccupied and insensitive to others. It really stings to admit this, especially because I want to think of myself as a "caring person." Rather than acceptantly exploring this habit within me, it is much easier to blast away at others.

Needs other people's "sins" in order to dodge oneself. Related to the previous two points, this is an interesting and essential characteristic of judgmentalism. Stated simply, judgmental thinking is "addicted" to other people's sin or destructive behavior. Judgmentalism finds its identity in

18

what it *is not.* It defines itself by what it is reacting against. If there were no one around to condemn, judgmentalism wouldn't know what to do with itself. Anxiety quickly arises when there is nothing to judge.

It is a sad commentary on any of us whenever our identity comes from what we *don't* do. In order to feel acceptable to ourselves, we must constantly find someone we are *not like.* We *need* their problems in order to keep going. We've got to have something on which to focus. A friend of mine provides an interesting illustration of this. Sinking deeper and deeper into alcoholism, he would, of necessity, find someone who was in worse shape than he was in. "Now that," he would say, "is an alcoholic." His drinking associates became less and less functional because he always needed to find someone in really bad shape. His identification of a "real alcoholic" became more and more pitiful. Without someone worse off than he, he would have had to look at himself.

Such a judgmental maneuver is characteristic of a television evangelist who objects constantly to the issue of sexuality. This preoccupation may well be a detour away from his own sexual behavior. His obsession with sexual promiscuity may find its way into every one of his sermons. Clearly, he projects his own dark side onto his congregation.

What would we do without "bad people"? They provide us with something to talk about. They are a focus for our energy. As an escape from self-exploration, they carry our shame for us. We *need* them to avoid ourselves.

Turns away from grace and acceptance of self and others. It would indeed be a sad day when religion has nothing to say once it quits judging things. Discussions of grace, freedom, love, compassion, and forgiveness are simply not as easy as discussions about who is doing what and why it is so wrong. When we are preoccupied with the judging of others, our attention is far removed from the liberation and life-changing power of acceptance.

I, personally, have never known anyone who has ever changed much as a result of condemnation. While we all need to be confronted or challenged at times, that is only half the story. Along with the judgment of our action must come an acceptance of our personhood. A nonjudgmental acceptance of the person behind the behavior is the backbone of effective counseling and psychotherapy. Stated in more religious terms, grace brings on the possibility of repentance. It is easy to scream at someone, "Change... change...change!" It is much harder to value and prize someone *while they are trying to change.* Conditional acceptance is easy to offer, but it does not have the revolutionary power that unconditional acceptance offers. This point about unconditional acceptance is conveyed powerfully in the following fictional story.

> A man who was entirely careless of spiritual things died and went to Hell. And he was much missed on earth by his old friends. His business manager went down to the gates of Hell to see if there were any chance of bringing him back. But, though he pleaded for the gates to be opened, the iron bars never yielded. His cricket captain went also and besought Satan to let him out just for the remainder of the season. But there was no response. His minister went also and argued, saying, "He was not altogether bad. Let him have another chance. Let him out just this once." Many other friends of his went also and pleaded with Satan saying, "Let him out. Let him out. Let him out." But when his mother came, she spoke no word of his release. Quietly, and with a strange catch in her voice,

20

she said to Satan, *"Let me in."* And immediately the great doors swung open upon their hinges. For love goes down through the gates of Hell and there redeems the damned."[3]

Avoids the anxiety of seeing life's complexities. One of the most important aspects of judgmental thinking is that it eliminates the complexity of predicaments. It is not interested in the situational factors or particular circumstances of anyone's actions. In short, it does not see any specific behavior in a context. Quite frankly, the context is irrelevant. Judgmentalism arrogantly brags about its ability to "call a spade a spade" or "tell it the way it is." It will not dare to lovingly enter the framework or background of someone's behavior. That is too confusing. While we may not condone or approve of a behavior, we need to *understand* the circumstances in which such a behavior arose.

This is why highly judgmental people make such terrible counselors. They are not willing to enter the depths of a true dilemma. It feels too unsafe, too scary. Also, they are not willing to invest the energy and time it takes to lovingly stand with someone *in their situation*. This journey would leave them feeling too helpless, maybe even without answers.

Rabbi Harold Kushner has some insightful words about the importance of simply being with someone in the face of hurt. His reference is to how little help was provided by Job's friends as they approached Job during his suffering and tragedy.

> Job needed sympathy more than he needed advice, even good and correct advice. There would be a time and place for that later. He needed compassion, the sense that others felt his pain, more than he needed

learned theological explanations about God's ways. He needed physical comforting, people sharing their strength with him, holding him rather than scolding him....He needed friends who would permit him to be angry, to cry and to scream, much more than he needed friends who would urge him to be an example of patience and piety to others. He needed people to say, "Yes, what happened to you is terrible and makes no sense," not people who would say, "Cheer up Job, it's not all that bad." That was where his friends let him down. The phrase "Job's comforters" has come into the language to describe people who mean to help, but who are more concerned with their own needs and feelings than they are with those of the other person, and so end up only making things worse.[4]

Loves "labels" as a form of security. The avoidance of ambiguity is often made possible by dichotomous thinking or black-and-white labels. Everything is divided into two mutually exclusive groups: right/wrong, for us/against us, masculine/feminine, brilliant/ignorant, weak/strong, secure/insecure. A judgmental mind ignores all grey areas, forgets about the exceptions to the rule, and eliminates all qualifications in its crusade of labeling. Subtleties are lost as perspectives are forced to fit a theoretical mold. Tags are put on all positions. A rush toward dismissal prevents any possibility of a deeper hearing of the issues. All perspectives must be put in a box, or placed in a particular camp.

Labels are at first appealing because they eliminate the plausibility of alternative claims. This helps manage anxiety. Life is convenient. A sense of mastery often accompanies this ability to place perspectives into "camps." "Fred? Oh, Fred is into that new age nonsense." "Brenda? Well, what can you expect from a New England liberal?" And on it goes. Soon after judgmentalism puts people under labels, it starts beating them with these labels.

In Summary

These, then, are some of our main characteristics when we become judgmental. This list certainly indicts me, and I strongly suspect it also describes others. It is easier to be less hostile toward the judgmental thinking in others when we can spot it in ourselves.

The terms "judgmental" and "authoritarian" are very closely related. Let's now turn our attention toward this important connection.

CHAPTER TWO

Anxiety and Authoritarian Thinking

I remember, in the early days of my teaching career, being caught off guard by an insightful and very difficult question. I spoke very rapidly as I dodged this inquiry. My avoidance maneuvering was probably obvious as my attitude became more rigid. The truth was that I didn't have the answer. In fact, I, too, was gripped by the question. What I needed to do, but seemed unable to do at the time, was simply say, "I don't know."

Unfortunately, it is a short step from being frightened to being dogmatic. A natural tendency, for most of us, when we feel threatened by insecurity, is to tighten the grip on whatever belief we hold. When our judgmental pronouncements lack modesty, they are most likely intended to tame the anxiety and insecurity lurking beneath us. When we speak about ultimate matters without the slightest bit of reservation, or rarely mention the limitations of human understanding, we are in a state of self-avoidance. Our tone lacks any sort of trembling, our declarations are made with

24

ease, and they claim a certainty unknown to most. Further, we may have little tolerance for doubt as we utter grandiose claims without any form of second-guessing. When others hear our self-assured comments, they may well be provoked to withdraw and say, "Wait a minute. It's just not as *obvious* as you say it is."

Judgmentalism often displays an intense need to deny, escape, and stamp out uncertainty and insecurity. Living in a diverse, pluralistic society is particularly difficult for judgmental thinkers. A diverse society brings with it a multitude of perspectives. As a result, judgmentalists often spend an enormous amount of unproductive time *in reaction* to other viewpoints. As certainties begin to fade, hostilities begin to grow. In an attempt to hide from insecurity, judgmentalists indulge in authoritarian thinking. In fact, authoritarian thinking may well be the primary characteristic of judgmentalism. Authoritarians are hard to approach.

It's important to remember that judgmental thinking is almost always controlled by outside factors. Judgmentalism reacts rather than responds. When we become judgmental, we are often controlled by the very groups we fight. Outside enemies control our agenda. We can't leave them alone. They determine our thinking in that we *must* rail against them. We become far more able to tell others what we are *against* than what we are *for*. We may feel pushed around and our paranoid defensiveness may snarl with yet another rebuke of something. We must condemn. Thus, we are not free to initiate, share, or offer our perspective. We are compulsively driven to convert anything that does not look like us!

The simple social fact of variety and diversity often creates a sense of inner rage within many judgmentalists. How dare life not conform to easy dualities! The only function of differing opinions is to confuse and perplex. Pluralism is demonic. Forget all the options! The illusion of multiple paths is part of the devil's road map. Rampages against "all those weird views out there" grow out of this internal need to order life into a right-or-wrong framework. Variety is hardly the spice of life when it comes to religious or ethical matters. Again, pluralism (the availability of a multitude of perspectives, lifestyles, and values from which to choose) is annoying to anyone who wants to think out of all-or-nothing categories. Judgmentalists will often go to great lengths to show that what "appears" to be a variety of options is actually an illusion. There really aren't that many choices.

Judgmentalism as Authoritarian Thinking

"Authoritarian" refers to a pattern of thinking, a perspective on life, or a way of perceiving the world. Being an "authoritarian" means always having a rigid mentality. While the beliefs of various authoritarians may differ, the underlying pattern or type of reasoning is largely identical.

Judgmentalism and authoritarianism are two sides of the same coin. But how do we describe authoritarian thinking? In characterizing it, we must be careful to pinpoint specific patterns of thought and behavior rather than to condemn the person behind them. It is very easy to become judgmental about authoritarian people. However, authoritarianism as a mental pattern and interpersonal sickness *does* need to be confronted.

To portray the authoritarian nature, we'll take each letter of the word to describe its character.

A bsence of spontaneity
U nderstanding other viewpoints is unnecessary
T ruth is singular and our group owns it
H urting others through dominance and force is justified
O rder takes priority over further exploration
R epitition of old ideas is superior to creativity
I ndividualism falls prey to "group think"
T urning away from the common viewpoint is betrayal
A mbiguity is an illusion
R epression is typical
I gnorance is reduced to willful disobedience
A nnouncing the truth eliminates dialogue
N ever admits faults and mistakes

Let's discuss each one of these traits in more detail.

Absence of spontaneity. Life becomes an obsessive-compulsive job. The same rules are used over and over again. The fact that these old ideas don't explain today's reality doesn't matter. When we are excessively afraid of life, the fear keeps us locked into the same old pattern. There is rarely anything creative or refreshing happening.

Ed is a good example of this absence of spontaneity. He has been defined by traditionalism and he is extremely leery of change. His life is dull, boring, and in desperate need of being embraced. Instead, he lives according to worn out rules that keep him depressed. Others do not hear him belly-laugh, play, enjoy unstructured conversations, or do anything "off the cuff." His life is strategically calculated in order to minimize all risk. Things simply *must* be familiar. If not, he becomes filled with panic. He believes he has some sort of "control" over reality. Repetition, conformity, "managing himself," and keeping everything in line are his primary concerns.

Ed believes the world is run by clear-cut laws and rules that are beyond exception. In a sense, Ed believes not that the laws exist for people, but that people exist for those laws. Ed comes across as stubborn, set in his ways, and hard-headed. His compassion runs low and his judgment runs high. His family, particularly his daughters, find his attitude and behavior nearly unbearable. "He never wants to have any fun," say his kids.

Spontaneity is lacking in Ed's life because of fear. The only way he knows to hold things together is with an iron grip. Poised, hyper, and afraid to relax, he lives his life holding his breath.

Understanding other viewpoints is unnecessary. Most of us have had the experience of trying to share a viewpoint with people who are unwilling, or perhaps unable, to even begin to see our perspective. They simply won't hear and won't try it on. Instead, they stay completely locked into their own angle. There is, of course, enormous arrogance and fear behind their narrow focus. We know how frustrating it can be to attempt communication with such people.

Yet we also need to remember that arrogance and fear are two pieces of the same puzzle. On the surface, of course, authoritarian viewpoints look like a crude form of arrogance. It's as if authoritarians are saying, "There is no difference between *my* reality and reality itself," or "The way I see it is the way it is." The equation of our own specific viewpoint, with all its limitations, distortions, and particularities, *with reality itself* is indeed an expression of conceit and hubris. However, it is also a frightened scramble to protect ourselves from clashing viewpoints. It's a retreat from pluralism or diversity. We act as if there's only one reality, and after a while, we believe it. As long as we associate with like-minded perspectives, our own outlook goes unchallenged.

Truth is singular and our group owns it. Understanding other viewpoints becomes unnecessary when we think the truth has arrived and is firmly in our grasp. Our own clan has an absolute hold on ultimate matters. We *know*. We reinforce each other's certainty by acknowledging the same things. Staying in our own group (and disconnecting with others) becomes essential if we are to remain completely sure of what we believe. The "world" is reduced to our own group's activities. Outside influences are avoided like the plague.

Sociologists call this group self-centeredness ethnocentricity. All other perceptions of reality are harshly evaluated by our group's measuring stick. Rarely are other viewpoints seen as simply "different." Instead, they are "weird," "off the wall," or "completely irrational."

Hurting others through dominance and force is justified. When we are *so sure* that we own the truth, we often feel justified to clobber other people with it. Their individual freedom is overlooked and their choice is dismissed. Conversations are turned into power struggles in which we must conquer opposing viewpoints. Our own beliefs must be protected even if it means hurting others' feelings.

Cruelty and interpersonal insensitivity are especially difficult to challenge when they claim to be religiously justified. We then think we are empowered to make prophetic pronouncements against others. We are defending the faith and telling it like it is. Others must conform to our sense of morality. They are not respected as persons. They become sinners, deadbeats, drunkards, and whores. They are consumed by

29

our labels. We have their number, and because we are so righteous, we are entitled to push them around.

This, of course, is an old story in religious history. The same faith that proclaims peace and nonviolence has been used to oppress, dominate, and force others to submit. Horrifying things have been done in the name of God. Leslie Weatherhead, a leading clergyman of the 20th century, reminds us of this very well.

> Narrow-minded and intolerant men have often desired that those who differed from them should be tortured, or, at any rate suffer, e.g., the members of the Inquisition, and the medieval barons who built their dining halls just above the dungeons so that the groans of tortured prisoners might enhance the pleasures of the diners at their revels and orgies of triumph.[5]

While we may not physically persecute people of a different viewpoint, the emotional abuse of them is often apparent. We tell ourselves that when they disagree with us they are spitting in the face of God. Consequently, we are justified in rebuking them. Our labels become our clubs and they are burned at the stake of our judgments. To our own way of thinking, we have divine sanction to be intolerant.

I remember working once with a particular family in which the father's religious belligerence made communication almost impossible. Seeing himself as the holy man of the family, he did not have to burden himself with the tiresome struggle of listening to his wife or children. The family was thrashed by the Bible, told how to live, and expected to conform to all his private ideas about life.

Order takes priority over further exploration. While finding a sense of order to our world is important to most of us, anxiety can easily push us toward an excessive demand for mental tidiness. Everything must be figured out and put in its place. All the messy, unexplained facets of life must be shoved into categories. Maintaining the old, secure way of looking at things, even when it doesn't fit our experience, is upheld over admitting uncertainties. In relationships, this comes across as: Your experience must fit my preconceptions! If your experience does not seem to match my existing interpretations, then I will twist, minimize, or change it so that it is compatible with my ideas about the world. Nothing is going to shake the stability or security of my cozy little world view. No matter what your experience seems to be, I will put it in categories manageable for me.

This is especially common when we meet someone whose suffering we cannot understand. Rather than recognizing their pain and simply admitting that we don't know why this is happening to them, "explanations" are frequently offered. It becomes very clear after a while that the explanation is a frantic attempt to hold together our own viewpoint, rather than to comfort the person in pain. In fact, our "explanation" for their suffering, as Harold Kushner points out so well, may even be cruel.[6] We may end up blaming the victim, somehow suggesting that the suffering person brought this tragedy on him or herself.

Not so long ago, I lost my wife in a tragic automobile accident. This same accident nearly took my life as well. As I was recuperating for several months in the hospital, I appreciated the manner in which so many people's hearts reached out to me. Some people very wisely realized that "interpretations" as to why this had all happened were simply not satisfying or adequate. With a loving presence, they embraced

31

my confusion and did not back away from the struggles this raised for my own religious faith.

Others, however, were extremely uncomfortable with the questions this experience provoked. In fact, I could see their own anxiety levels start to rise. Swiftly following this elevation of anxiety was an attempt to quickly offer explanations, *any* explanation, that would restore the security of their thinking. What was abundantly clear was this: Their answers were for them, not for me. The fox of doubt had threatened the security of *their* henhouse. This fox must quickly be eliminated. After all, even unsatisfying answers were better than no answers. The security of their religious worldview must be protected at all costs. So the primary task was protecting an old way of thinking rather than standing with me in my uncertainty.

It must be stressed that these were often very well-intentioned individuals. They were simply frightened, and this fear led them to cling to religious ideas that minimized or downplayed the problem. Often they did not realize that it was their own fear of doubt they were trying to fix, rather than my particular dilemma. My questions and confusions had triggered their own. Unwilling to face and explore the many unsettled mysteries within their own psyche, how could they possibly hear mine?

This excessive need for order is why many of us turn to a professional counselor or psychotherapist. In effective counseling, we have an opportunity to face our anxiety and insecurity without an immediate need to get rid of it. The therapist is not trying to talk us out of it, tell us it's no big deal, or quickly explain it in such a way that it is no longer a problem. In helpful counseling, the focus is on our struggle and not on the therapist's need to keep his or her worldview intact.

Prepackaged answers usually *sound* prescribed. They temporarily make life "manageable," but they ignore the underlying anxiety with which we all must deal. They come out of shallow waters and refuse to walk with a person into greater depths. Again, they are not designed to provide comfort. Instead, they are used to kill anxiety.

A person I know recently sought pastoral counseling from a church she had been attending. She had gone through an extremely rocky marriage, full of turmoil, abuse, and complications. She worried as to how she could possibly provide her minister with an overview of what had been going on the past several years. She was currently separated from her husband, very much afraid of him, and unwilling to go back into a relationship in which her children, as well as she, would live in perpetual fear.

When she met with the minister, she tried to describe the conditions under which she and her husband met, and offered what she thought was pertinent information about each of their families of origin. One thing was very clear to her: she was caught up in a very confusing, perplexing situation in which simple answers were impossible to find. She had tried to see life from everyone's angle—her kids', her husband's, and her own.

Much to her dismay, she soon discovered that this minister seemed rather uninterested in the complicated details and confusing aspects of her situation. He seemed focused on one thing only— had her husband been unfaithful? Did she have biblical grounds for a divorce? All of the complex issues surrounding abuse, communication, family dynamics, psychospiritual compatibility, and so on, were reduced to this one burning preoccupation: Did she have the "right" to divorce? The "caregiver" had no interest in walking with her through the ambivalent feelings, mixed thoughts, and alternative explanations for what may have happened to her marriage. All of that was beside the point. Essentially, he was saying to her, "Look, lady, I'm not interested in what *you* call a struggle, nor in what may *seem* like confusion to you. Underneath all that is a clear-cut answer I must give you. After all, you came to me for an answer. By providing you with a simple answer, I am able to keep my own little worldview secure."

This type of "counseling" is dehumanizing. We are not treated as the complex creatures we are. Instead, the helper's own need for order gets in the way.

Repetition of old ideas is superior to creativity. Always thinking in prepackaged ways, the authoritarian's capacity for creative thinking is nearly impoverished. For instance, in theology, if we see our task as the memorizing, cataloging, and factualizing of life, the delicate issues will go painfully uninterpreted. Stale, boring, unrelated perspectives push many people to live out of two worlds.

Closely related to judgmentalism is rigid thinking. When judgmentalists are questioned, they typically shout, tighten their argument in a defensive posture, then try to intimidate. Rigidity of thought often provokes insults, ridicule, and sometimes physical violence. Dialogue is rarely pleasant or stimulating. The most noticeably lacking characteristic is mutual respect. There is little, if any, value placed on the rights of other people.

This excessively rigid thinking style of judgmentalists certainly manifests itself in the sterile, prepackaged perspectives it manufactures. When we do not take our objectors seriously, we lack relevance to the world around us. The "same old material" is espoused in a contrived manner, even when it does not deal with the deeper needs of our lives.

This almost always leads to compartmentalized living, because the rules in our heads have little, if anything, to do with the streets on which we live. Rigid thought produces rigid rules. Rigid rules, in turn, produce people with barren emotional lives. We may experience a chronic, low-grade depression as we mourn the loss of an authentic, spontaneous self. We feel what we are *supposed* to feel. Looking within, attempting to embrace our perplexing emotional lives, requires a flexible mentality.

We pay a heavy price for this anti-introspective mindset. Because we are shut off from the unacceptable aspects of our emotional lives, we block any flow of grace. And by not facing ourselves, we increase our judgments of others. For instance, we may insist on viewing "sin" as external behavior because this surface-level focus keeps us from looking at the hurts and wounds beneath the very behavior we are condemning. Ignorant of our own inner life, we bomb and blast the enemy. But we never name the underlying hurt that keeps pushing us to attack.

Individualism falls prey to "group think." Authoritarian thinking typically has a profound distrust of individual exploration. Instead, our thoughts must be "lined up" with an entire group's perspective. There is normally very little tolerance for the doubts or questions of a struggling individual. Consequently, self-distrust and an unquestioned loyalty to the group are typical of authoritarians.

Submitting to an objective, group standard, even when it does not make sense in one's private world, is a major feature of authoritarianism. Personal doubts or questions must be abandoned. The collective consensus of the group acts as an anti-anxiety medication, calming the worries of individual consciousness. The group's teaching takes on an ontological status, as if it were built into reality itself. It moves beyond collective opinion to indubitable fact. It is part of the very structure of reality. To think outside the group's rigid boundaries is to engage in non-sense at best, or blasphemy at worse.[7]

Turning away from the common viewpoint is betrayal. To disagree or differ from the prevailing viewpoint is considered treachery. Because individual differences are not respected, any sort of departure from the abiding norm is highly threatening. In fact, it simply won't be tolerated. The differing individual is typically ridiculed or shamed back into submission. Again, he or she is warned of the awesome dangers of trusting one's own individual perspective.

Authoritarian groups are stuck together in a gooey mass of false togetherness. Genuine intimacy, which necessitates the development of two or more separate individuals sharing one another's reality, is impossible. Fear and control eliminate the possibility of autonomy. Group members are what family therapist Murray Bowen frequently calls "undifferentiated," bonded together to avoid the anxieties of being an individual. Authoritarian leaders are often masters at setting up the equation: to disagree with me is to disrespect and betray me. Many of us simply don't know how to handle the guilt that disagreement generates.

In many authoritarian, highly controlling families, it is frequently communicated to children that their primary role is to make mom and dad happy. In fact, they may well grow up to believe that this is their chief task, the main reason they came into this world. To want a life of their own is to be selfish and ungrateful. To seek independence is to betray the system. In a grossly distorted manner, the parent-child relationship is reversed, with children taking care of parents rather than parents being there for their kids. The children feel responsible for their parents' feelings, their parents' happiness, and even their parents' marriage. As parents want their children to fulfill all of their unmet needs, the kids become prisoners of dad and mom's unhappiness.

Ambiguity is an illusion. One of the most appealing fairy tales in authoritarian thinking is that there really is no such thing as ambiguity. Things simply have one meaning, and all uncertainty results from a lack of information. Something may *seem* to be ambiguous, but this is only because of our own ignorance. Life is clear-cut, without grey areas, and only one-way. If it does not appear this way, the problem is obviously the inadequacy of our own thinking.

It's tough to move out of this childhood consciousness and embrace the complications of being an adult human being. Sometimes, it does indeed seem as if there are two or three "right" answers rather than one. At other times, it seems as if all answers are wrong. Those who have allowed themselves to experience a moral dilemma understand this.

I have friends who are experiencing, for the first time, the awesome task of raising a child. I hear their frustrations and confusions as they struggle to do the "right" thing. I am reminded of the wonderfully insightful words of developmental psychologist Robert Gould as he describes the ambiguities of being a mother.

> In her daily experience with a child, a mother's time is not her own. She has to respond constantly to unclear verbal and preverbal demands from her child. Often she has no idea what to do; many times no good solution is available, so she'll suffer guilt and anxiety no matter what she does. The child constantly explores the boundaries of her patience and power. When the child's control lapses, her own control is required. She

must consider using force on a helpless human being who sometimes invades her bodily privacy and psychological integrity like a monstrous, consuming enemy. She deals with the world of child rearing, where hundreds of experts give contradictory advice; the outcome can't be measured for fifteen to twenty years. She has to process this advice through her intuition and a constant stream of her own childhood memories dredged up by her child's dilemmas. And she must do all this with others—mother, mother-in-law, neighbors and schoolteachers—looking over her shoulder, marking her report card, measuring her against their own standards. Though it would be a relief to give up and follow some set of packaged rules, she must dare to be different—the fate of her child depends on her decisions. Besides, no set of rules seems exactly right.[8]

These observations point very well to that uncertain element in adult thinking and behaving. While a world without ambiguity is a powerful wish of childhood, it must be gradually abandoned in order to live an authentic life.

Repression is typical. Part of authoritarian thinking is a very rigid and unbending image of ourselves. This inflexible portrait, or what psychoanalyst Karen Horney called an "idealized self,"[9] becomes the controlling image through which we allow feelings and thoughts to enter our awareness. In other words, only feelings that are consistent with our self-image are allowed. If my idealized self tells me that I am a man without fear, I will rename or flatly deny any feelings of fear I might legitimately have. That feeling doesn't match my fearless self-image, so it has to go.

As we can easily see, it doesn't take long for an uncompromising self-image to chase away unwanted feelings.

Those feelings are blocked or repressed. Thus, we become strangers to ourselves. We are so preoccupied with what we are *supposed* to feel that we ignore what we *really* feel.

Again, this idealized self is born out of the imagination and quite impossible to actualize. No one could possibly live up to the standards. It is a romanticized portrait built upon exaggerated self-expectations. The idealized self is above the traffic of everyday reality. Horney describes a person who chases the idealized self as follows.

> He feels what he *should* feel, wishes what he *should* wish, likes what he *should* like. In other words, the tyranny of the should drives him frantically to be something different from what he is or could be. And in his imagination he is different—so different, indeed, that his real self fades and pales even more.[10]

Trying to live within a restrictive, suffocating, rigid conception of life and ourselves always involves enormous denial. We ignore aspects of our own experience that do not conform to our elevated image of ideal personhood. The result is incongruence, the process of becoming a stranger to ourselves. The real self, consisting of our actual feelings and experience, becomes twisted, distorted, and stretched into a mold of the appropriate self. The end result of this censorship activity is self-alienation and ignorance of our real needs, desires, and dispositions toward life. The unhealthy trick, of course, is to somehow maintain the false image. This requires enormous energy and work. We must somehow falsify reality and discard all disturbing evidence to the contrary. Embodying perfection must somehow overshadow our all-too-human tendencies. Our real self is perceived as an annoying intruder. The idealized self is protected with the same energetic fervor with which a parent protects a newborn.

I have struggled with this problem of an idealized self as I have become more and more involved in personal growth and mental health. Because I have read about "appropriate anger," "thriving self-esteem," or "resolved grief," I sometimes convey my emotions only in "healthy" ways. My own standards have backed me into a corner. I say that I'm feeling what I think I *should* feel. Wanting to hide any dysfunctional or neurotic qualities, my self-presentation is carefully monitored and even censored. My feelings then become more prescribed than real.

Ignorance is reduced to willful disobedience. When we question an authoritarian's claim, our question is not treated as a sincere desire to understand. Instead, we don't understand *because we don't want to understand.* In other words, we are rebelling, not questioning. Our doubts are treated as a revolt or a rebellion. Our questions are not given dignity. On the contrary, they are reduced to a willful desire to remain in the dark. Our inquiring mind is seen as just a disguise for a deceitful heart. We don't have an ignorance problem; we have an impurity problem.

This is a handy way for authoritarian groups to shame their members into submission. Complete clarity, they say, is always available. The problem is that we simply don't want to understand badly enough. If we *really* wanted to comprehend, the truth would unfold immediately.

Announcing the truth eliminates dialogue. The truth, for authoritarians, is final, certain, and in no need of further discussion. We need not talk about it, polish it, or work with it. It stops, rather than promotes, dialogue. This, of course, is why it is so difficult to "explore" things with authoritarians. Rigid repetition of "captured" truth often prevents creative investigation.

The problem, of course, is that many things, such as art and literature, have inexhaustible meanings. At various moments or stages of our lives, we "see" different things in them. Authoritarians do not recognize the beauty in this. All things are reduced to one meaning, so our task is merely to memorize what has already been said before.

Never admits faults and mistakes. An authoritarian mentality refuses to acknowledge or own its own limitations. The words "I was wrong" or "I'm sorry" do not fall from an authoritarian's mouth. He or she must be infallible. Beneath the stiff pride, however, is a very fragile, insecure ego afraid to admit *any* sort of inadequacy. In fact, authoritarians do not have enough self-acceptance to be able to admit their faults and still be okay as people. They have backed themselves into a corner in which they must always be right. Anything short of this would devastate their self-image.

Because we can never be wrong, finding fault in others becomes a mandatory, full-time task. We simply *must* locate the fault somewhere outside of ourselves. Enormous energy is put into making sure that someone else is blamed. Afraid to be human, we waste much effort and time assigning blame to others, when it would be so much easier to simply own our own faults.

Coping with Authoritarians

As we have seen, tolerating critical, authoritarian people can be extremely difficult. If we have been wounded by judgmental thinking, we probably carry some anger about that hurt. After all, our boundaries have been violated and we may feel disrespected and invaded. When we are judged from a distance, without any attempt to understand us, we often recoil.

How can we find a way of protecting ourselves, and even nurturing ourselves, in the middle of a judgmental assault? How do we relate to authoritarianism without falling into its intolerance? How do we maintain our own composure when we bump into judgmental belligerence? What guidelines help us stay free from a narrow-minded trap? Here are some suggestions.

1. **REMEMBER, IN ADVANCE, THE MANNER OF AUTHORITARIAN THINKING.** We need not be surprised by pulverizing judgments, convenient categories, and insulting labels. After all, this is the nature of authoritarian thinking. Rigid, all-or-nothing pronouncements *will be* a part of the authoritarian thought world. We need not be shocked by it. Instead, we can brace ourselves for it.

2. **ENCOURAGE SITUATIONS IN WHICH A CONFRONTATION WITH DIFFERENT VIEWPOINTS IS PRACTICALLY INEVITABLE.** When we bump into well-intentioned representatives of alternative perspectives, we may begin to loosen our conviction that we *own* the truth. Again, the simple fact that several viewpoints are available starts to challenge the idea that any *one* of them has a monopoly on truth.

3. **CONSTANTLY INVITE BLACK-OR-WHITE THINKERS TO TAKE ON THE PERSPECTIVES OF OTHERS.** We can ask authoritarian thinkers how other people have arrived at their point of view. If authoritarians start to see the context of other people's lives and thoughts, they may begin to recognize that their own thinking, also, emerges in a particular context and is limited. Authoritarians are weak on perspective-taking

skills. They need practice in placing themselves in another's frame of reference. Perhaps they will begin to see that all thought, even ideas about ultimate matters, occurs in a specific and limited location.

4. **REMEMBER THAT AUTHORITARIANS ARE OFTEN ABUSIVE BECAUSE THEY ARE ANXIOUS.** A craving for security can be similar to an addiction. In fact, "absolute certainty" can function like a drug of choice. Authoritarians often believe that even a small cog in their grand conceptual scheme will ruin everything. Consequently, enormous hostility occurs when we ask them probing questions. They do not want to rethink their world. Probably none of us delights in the loss of security that accompanies a challenge to our belief system. But for authoritarians, the challenge is unbearable. Therefore, fighting overthrows discussing; conquering overshadows sharing; and winning means more than searching.

5. **REMEMBER THAT WE ARE NOT RESPONSIBLE FOR CHANGING AN AUTHORITARIAN'S PATTERN OF THINKING.** We need not fall prey to being a martyr or missionary for open-mindedness. We do not have the power to convert anyone into a flexible thinker. Besides, trying to "force" open-mindedness is a contradiction in terms. We can't control the controllers. Simply taking care of ourselves so that *we* are not controlled is a full-time job. Many authoritarians will indeed continue their rigid and abusive thought patterns. Our energy needs to be invested in building our own shield of independence and autonomy.

We can also remember that we do not have to come to a harmonious conclusion with authoritarian thinking. Some people's assumptions and interpersonal style will defy any possibility of peaceful relations. What is telling us that we *must* make peace with them? It is probably our own unrealistic expectations.

6. **REMEMBER THAT IMITATING AUTHORITARIAN BELLIGERENCE WILL BE ENORMOUSLY TEMPTING.** The human impulse to meet aggression with aggression will probably emerge. As we have seen, being tolerant of intolerance is a difficult task. The awareness, in advance, that we may experience a combative reaction from authoritarians will probably provide us with greater choice as to how we respond. Put simply, we will be less prone to react when we are not ambushed.

7. **REMEMBER TO LOOK AT OUR OWN TENDENCIES TOWARD AUTHORITARIAN THINKING.** Once again, authoritarian, judgmental thinking arises in all of us at times. Are we inflexible in our "demand for flexibility"? Are we being narrow-minded by *insisting* that everyone be open-minded? Complete dismissal of people, once their authoritarian roots have been exposed, is very tempting but not interpersonally healing or peacemaking. While we may see the severe limitations of authoritarian thinking, we need not deny it the very choice it is attempting to deny us. Put directly, people have the right to choose close-mindedness or even ignorance.

8. **REMEMBER THAT WHEN AUTHORITARIAN THINKING REACTS TO OUR UNCERTAINTY, THIS REACTION IS PROBABLY BASED ON A DENIAL OF ITS OWN UNCERTAINTY.** Our doubts may be their doubts. In fact, this may be what authoritarian thinking is fighting—the uncertainty within itself. Unable to admit this, it externalizes the doubt and attacks it in others. What we cannot accept within ourselves we project onto anyone who raises disturbing questions.

9. **REMEMBER THAT AUTHORITARIAN THINKING SEES A CHALLENGE TO ITS PERSPECTIVE AS A CHALLENGE TO ITS IDENTITY.** We all tend to resist examining who we are. Authoritarian

thinking frequently believes that all identity issues have been nailed down, so further questions are both unnecessary and annoying. All problems concerning "who we are" have been solved. The case is closed. A challenge to a perspective is perceived as a challenge to personhood. As C. S. Lewis has frequently commented, most of the time that we are defending God, we are really defending ourselves.

10. ENCOURAGE INDIVIDUALS TO ASSOCIATE WITH REFERENCE GROUPS THAT HAVE A TOLERANCE FOR RAISING QUESTIONS, EXPLORING OPTIONS, AND WONDERING ABOUT ISSUES. A "new way of thinking" needs a supportive influence if it is to be maintained. As sociologist Peter Berger has often pointed out so well, a major change in perspective will not last long if it is not fueled by conversational partners. The old, familiar way of seeing the world will creep back in and the new, more flexible angle will be sabotaged by anxiety. Ideas, as much as emotions, need support.

11. REMEMBER TO REFLECT A COMFORT WITH DOUBT AND A RELAXED ATTITUDE TOWARD UNCERTAINTY. The fact that we do not panic over unanswerable questions models both a healthy faith and an acceptance of human limitations. Mature faith does not need to avoid, fight, or always conquer doubt. We can express a commitment that does not demand demonstrable proof and a conviction that does not necessitate certainty. There is a tremendous relief in grasping that finite minds can never totally grasp the infinite. The burden of "perfectly figuring out the whole show" becomes a much more modest quest.

12. REMEMBER TO SPEAK OUT OF OUR OWN EXPERIENCE RATHER THAN CONSTANTLY "SPEAKING FOR" AN ENTIRE GROUP OR TRADITION. No one "owns" *the* orthodox point of view. We need to disclaim any pretensions of having imprisoned the

truth; however, there is no need to apologize for learnings from our personal experience. Perhaps, as Carl Rogers used to point out, we have been so busy telling our experience what *it* means that we have never let it tell us what *we* mean. Every human being needs to ask, "What do I really believe?" It is always tempting to let external authorities interpret our experience for us. Often, we then end up forcing our experience into structures of interpretation that simply don't fit.

13. **REMEMBER THE EXTREMELY LIMITED VALUE OF DEBATE WHEN IT COMES TO VALUE QUESTIONS OR TO RELIGIOUS AND SPIRITUAL MATTERS.** How many people change their thinking, much less their attitudes, about important value questions as a result of rigorous debate and argumentation? It is normally the quality of our lives, and not the flawlessness of our logic, that influences others. Debate about religious and moral issues promotes defensiveness more often than understanding.

14. **HELP PERSONS REINTERPRET THEIR PAST WORLD FROM THE STANDPOINT OF THEIR NEW OUTLOOK.** Old perspectives, beliefs, and values need to be integrated into our present location, rather than being allowed to dangle in the past. Some people do not know what to do with their previous experience. It is important that they find ways of fitting it into a more comprehensive interpretation of their lives. We need to see continuities, themes, and unified connections in our lives. Otherwise, we live in disjointed segments of time. Changing our outlook does not have to involve denying our pilgrimage. Or, as Peter Berger has said, "To change one's mind is not to take back one's life."[11]

15. **REMEMBER THAT BEING OPEN-MINDED DOES NOT MEAN ACCEPTING PERPETUAL ABUSE.** Allowing ourselves to undergo abuse is a sign of low self-esteem. Judgmental abuse is no

47

exception. We have every right to protect our boundaries. If authoritarian thinkers attempt to invade those boundaries, and therefore become poisonous for us, we probably need to cut off contact with them. Boundary violation is always dysfunctional, even if it's done in the name of moral or religious supremacy. One acid test for religious or value commitments is how much they respect the freedom of others.

In Summary

We cannot change authoritarian thinking, except in ourselves. If we attempt to revise others' perspectives, we fall into the same control madness we have seen in them. Authoritarian thinking can be abusive, belligerent, rigid and quite obnoxious. It can have a toxic interpersonal style. Most of us can tolerate it in only limited doses. Otherwise, we get hooked by its aggressive bait and end up in an unfortunate and unnecessary catfight.

The crucial issue is self-care. We need to "stay underneath our own skin" and realize that we are responsible only for ourselves. Put directly, we need to allow other people to be judgmentally crazy without getting caught up in that craziness. A stubborn refusal to allow other people's bizarre notions to infiltrate our perspective, along with a realization that insecurity is at the bottom of authoritarian thinking, will help equip us to cope with judgmental abuse.

CHAPTER THREE

Making Judgments vs.
Being Judgmental

Two people, Frank and Ted, are talking about a very frightening event in their neighborhood. A young woman was raped over the weekend. Frank declares that this is a despicable thing that provokes enormous anger in him. After all, he has a younger sister who lives in this part of town. Ted then tells Frank that he shouldn't be so "judgmental."

"How can you possibly be tolerant of something like that?" Frank retorted.

"I just know," said Ted, "that part of my own spiritual commitment is to not judge."

The comments expressed between Frank and Ted lead to a lot of confused thinking. Surely there must be a difference between making judgments and being judgmental. Did Frank not have the right to feel ethically outraged by this violent act? Of course he did. It is perfectly appropriate to negatively evaluate actions and behavior that bring hurt, damage, or pain to another human being. In fact, to *not* react to such a behavior is to have a very numbed conscience.

In a retaliation against judgmentalism, however, some individuals have insisted upon judging nothing. All things, they say, are acceptable or somehow a part of the scheme of things. All of us have our private opinions, but someone else's behavior is none of our business. The worst thing imaginable is intolerance. In fact, intolerance is seen as the only taboo in a very diverse world. The worst thing that can befall anyone is to be seen as "judgmental."

Sometimes this all-embracing attitude is grounded or justified in various forms of religion or philosophy. A theme frequently emerging in "New Age" philosophy or belief is the thinking that "everything is as it should be." When I have been anxious about the day's activities, I have often been told by New Age friends that everything will happen exactly as it is *supposed* to happen. If I could only see from a larger framework, they say, I would know that all things have their place. From a cosmic angle, everything is a piece of the ultimate puzzle.

The end result of this philosophy, however, is an ethical neutrality and a moral indifference. A desire to "not come down on anything" places us in a world without convictions, a place where all standards are completely private, and a situation in which society is nearly impossible. One morality is just as good as the next. Mother Teresa and Hitler simply show us different forms of self-expression. It's a world in which we need not be outraged when a woman is raped; we need not call the death of a five year old a "tragedy"; and we are "unenlightened" when we call the random killing of a thirty-year-old "evil."

The confusion here is between judging behavior or ideas and being judgmental about people. But what can be said about this important distinction?

Healthy Judgments vs. Judgmentalism: Eight Distinctions

Let's examine eight very important differences between making judgments and being judgmental.

Healthy Judgment	Judgmentalism
Healthy judgment is the rational process of evaluating evidence and coming to well-thought-out decisions.	Judgmentalism is "emotional reasoning" that makes snap decisions based on superficial evidence.
Healthy judgment is the necessary outcome of reflective, careful thinking, and the mark of a mind unafraid to decide.	Judgmentalism is the outcome of unreflective, careless thinking, and is the mark of a mind afraid to think analytically.
Healthy judgment soberly recognizes unresolved problems with our own viewpoint.	Judgmentalism refuses to recognize the "blinders" or limitations of our viewpoint.
Healthy judgment includes a willingness to change our mind.	Judgmentalism involves an unwillingness to change our mind.
Healthy judgment refuses to distrust another's motives unless we have solid evidence for doing so.	Judgmentalism presumes to know other persons' motives without reasonable evidence.

Healthy judgment involves holding to moral and religious concepts with charity and tolerance toward those who differ.	Judgmentalism clings tenaciously to moral and religious concepts with disrespect and intolerance toward those who differ.
Healthy judgment entails a denunciation of hurtful *behavior* or erroneous *ideas*.	Judgmentalism denounces the *person* who adheres to erroneous ideas or destructive behavior.
Healthy judgment involves a concern for others.	Judgmentalism is not concerned for others.

Let's look, in more detail, at these key differences.

Making a healthy judgment is a calm, sober insistence upon looking at all the evidence before reaching a conclusion. Healthy judgments normally take some *time*. They are weighed out, evaluated, and thought about carefully. Healthy judgments attempt to fairly examine as many factors as possible. They refuse to make mental jumps or careless castigations.

If a problem or issue does not trigger a great deal of emotion for us, most of us are capable of making healthy judgments. A decision as to which school to attend, which house to buy, or which insurance policy is best are all familiar examples. We *want* to be cautious and conscientious.

Judgmentalism, as a mentality, however, is based on a reactionary protest to something. It is "emotional reasoning" that allows clear thinking no room to navigate amid our colliding feelings. It does not seem to care that it lacks solid evidence. It is a knee-jerk opinion.

Much of the time, this emotional reasoning is based on

some sort of hurt we have experienced in the past. Someone then says or does something that triggers this unpleasant memory and we automatically strike out or want to "write them off." This is often done instantly and unconsciously.

An example of this can be taken from my psychology classes. When Sigmund Freud is introduced, some students almost immediately recoil. Freud, for them, is both a chauvinist and a man utterly preoccupied with sex. Because of his evaluation of women, the man has no truth to speak whatsoever! Even his name conjures up emotional reactions. The conclusion is drawn that because he had *some* sexist attitudes, *all* of his theories are invalid and not worth investigating.

Other examples, of course, could be used. I remember, as an undergraduate student studying philosophy and religion, not wanting to hear or read about *any* of John Calvin's religious views because he was responsible for Servetus being burned at the stake. Anyone, I thought, with that kind of intolerance is not worthy of attention. It took a while to realize that this one act, dreadful as it was, did not eliminate all possibility that Calvin might have some insights about other matters. My instant dismissal of Calvin had to be reexamined.

Another characteristic of healthy judgments is that it is not driven by fear. Instead, it is a careful expression of a mind unafraid to decide. It does not remain forever suspended because it recognizes that choosing one thing means denying another. Going to San Francisco on vacation means not going to Florida. Taking French this semester means not taking German. Decision means "cutting off" or letting go of some possibilities while affirming others.

Judgmentalism, on the other hand, is driven by a fear of carefully examining evidence and thinking analytically. Judgmentalism is too impulsive to carefully look at all the

choices. It tends to be unreflective and careless. Again, it does not have time to withhold its opinion. Plus, that's too much work and requires too much energy.

Healthy judgment recognizes the unresolved problems with our own viewpoint. It knows its limits and has some intellectual humility. It does not parade its view as if that view were without limitations. It admits having "blinders" or areas in which it does not see the whole picture. It quits demanding certainty in order to have conviction. It lives with a healthy skepticism about its own "absolute certainty." In the back of our minds, the words of 17th-century philosopher Blaise Pascal still make sense:

> This is our true state; this is what makes us incapable of certain knowledge and of absolute ignorance. We sail within a vast sphere, ever drifting in uncertainty, driven from end to end. When we think to attach ourselves to any point and to fasten to it, it wavers and leaves us; and if we follow it, it eludes our grasp, slips past us, and vanishes forever. Nothing stays for us. This is our natural condition, and yet most contrary to our inclination; we burn with desire to find solid ground and an ultimate sure foundation whereon to build a tower reaching to the Infinite. But our whole groundwork cracks, and the earth opens to abysses.[12]

By contrast, judgmentalism refuses to recognize any problems or limitations with its own viewpoint. With intellectual arrogance, it insists on absolute certainty. If it is challenged, it frequently reacts with hostility toward the questioner. It is proud of its conviction and expects immediate agreement from others.

As an undergraduate student, I remember a couple of times when our university was visited by individuals who made enormously grandiose claims about ethics and religious truth. They would describe how they had sifted through and carefully scrutinized every possible world view. Yes, they had looked at Eastern as well as Western religious perspectives, and had investigated all agnostic, atheistic, deistic, and fideistic angles. Having conducted this careful, tedious study of thousands of years of thought, having "objectively considered" all potential world views, it "just so happened" that their view was the only one that made any sense. Their perspective alone was valid.

This is an embarrassing illustration of being out of touch with our own limitations. To make these claims, after having visited the millions of volumes in a university library, is absurd. This is an example of the denial of humanness, a display to avoid insecurity, and an uncaring attitude toward those who differ. To suggest that our explorations are completely objective, comprehensive, and exhaustive is to promote a very unfortunate form of intellectual pride. Besides, for those of us who claim that we believe what we do because of "an exhaustive exploration of the data," there are millions whose lives illustrate that we believe what we do primarily because of what is plausible in our sociohistorical location. We have every right to believe what we do; let's just not kid ourselves by saying that we "arrived" here as a result of a completely objective, comprehensive search that has eliminated all alternatives.

Also, healthy judgment involves a willingness to change our mind. This means that right in the middle of an argument, we may turn an about face and say, "I believe you're right." While we may not see this happen very often, it *is* a possibility when we form healthy judgments. We simply see that another viewpoint explains more or makes more sense than ours. Because we are not arrogantly attached to "owning" the truth, we are then free to change our thinking as new evidence comes in. This does *not* mean that we lack convictions, nor does it mean that we have previously been an idiot. It simply means that we have new information, a new perspective, a better way of looking at something than before. In short, this kind of change is quite possible if we can keep our swollen or bruised egos out of the picture.

Healthy judgment refuses to distrust another's motives unless we have solid evidence for doing so. Judgmentalism, on the other hand, claims to be able to read people's minds. Judgmentalism *knows* what everyone's motive is, even when there is no reasonable evidence. It has secret information that it uses to clobber another.

Sometimes it is automatically assumed that when someone does something nice for us, he or she is "after something." When a man and woman talk, they must be planning an affair. When two men hug, they must be homosexual. The arrogance underlying our assumption to "know" all these things can be notorious. By "reading into" other people's behavior, we do harm to them.

Another characteristic of judgmentalism is that it clings so tenaciously to religious and moral concepts that it ends up disrespecting anyone who is different. Healthy judgment, by contrast, extends charity and respect to people who differ. Healthy judgment may indeed think that the *ideas* of someone are off-base, limited, or even dangerous. However, it extends a tolerance to the *person* beneath the ideas. It knows that giving an opposing viewpoint "air time" does not mean that we endorse it. Judgmentalism, on the other hand, is afraid even to hear the voice of another perspective. It cannot distinguish between respectfully listening to people and agreeing with them. When we are judgmental, other ideas are extremely dangerous and we are often paranoid about them. Superstitiously, we assume that merely hearing them will somehow cause us to be "taken over" by them. Out of fear, we disregard common courtesy. While healthy judgment is not afraid to condemn racism, sexism, dehumanizing attitudes, the exploitation of people, and other sinful practices, judgmentalism "plays God" in that it refuses to separate the person from his or her ideas and conduct.

And finally, whereas healthy judgment involves a concern for others, judgmentalism often has no concern whatsoever for the people it is condemning. Judgmentalism does not care if it hurts another's feelings. It is far more interested in winning the argument than in helping another human being. The irony once again, for judgmental thinking, is that people will not listen (no matter how convincing the argument) if they do not feel cared for.

In Summary

These, then, are some of the principal aspects of healthy judgment. Healthy judgment evaluates evidence carefully, is unafraid to decide, recognizes its own limitations, is willing to change its mind, refuses to distrust another's motives unless there is clear evidence for this suspicion, holds its convictions with charity and tolerance for others, separates behavior and ideas from the people who hold them, and involves a concern for others. These features are typically lacking in judgmentalism.

Let's now look at how to bolster and expand our ability to make healthy judgments without falling prey to judgmentalism.

CHAPTER FOUR

With an Open Mind and a Generous Heart

Eliminating all of our judgmentalism is a nice thought, but not a likely reality. Snap judgments, impatient criticisms, and unfair condemnations will indeed enter our thinking. We can make enormous progress in understanding and detoxifying them. We can cultivate an attitude of acceptance as a daily spiritual practice. Yet we will occasionally relapse into old patterns of unfriendly put-downs. Having a completely nonjudgmental idealized self is as dangerous as any other type of idealized self. We end up with harsh self-judgments or denial of our actual feelings.

Responding Rather Than Reacting to Others

One of the most significant aspects of nonjudgmental thinking is to clearly understand the differences between responding and reacting to life. Here are some important characteristics of responding.

R equires minding our own business
E ases others by offering them a space to be themselves
S eeks positive thoughts and not opportunities to judge
P ractices empathy
O wns our emotions and behavior as our responsibility
N urtures a sense of choice
D evelops an awareness of our own shortcomings
I gnores spicy, hearsay gossip
N ourishes grace for self and others
G ives people the benefit of the doubt

Let's examine, a little more carefully, each of these attributes.

How difficult it is for us to simply mind our own business! It is so easy to get snagged, hooked, or fixated on what someone else is doing. Even when it has nothing whatsoever to do with us, we focus on it. We are shocked, disturbed, upset, critical, or even obsessed with things we cannot even begin to control. We don't stop to ask ourselves *why* we are so preoccupied. Instead, we analyze, explore, criticize, and review another's actions as if we were his or her keeper.

A helpful habit when we notice this tendency is to routinely ask ourselves, "What has this to do with me?" This begins a detachment process in which our own emotions and thoughts are not completely bound up and controlled by another. Several years ago I remember hearing Albert Ellis say at a workshop, "We forget the most basic thing in life every day when we get up....Namely, many people we encounter are 'nuts.'" After I was no longer stunned or laughing at this interesting comment by one of our pioneer psychologists, I began to think about how true it is. I realized that of course I am going to bump into what seems unhealthy behavior to me. Am I going to react in an equally neurotic way by allowing it to affect and control my own emotional state? Am I going to be so shocked, angry, appalled, or disgusted that my own emotional peace is threatened? If I am not careful, my energies will be spent on fruitlessly processing the goings-on of others.

It is sometimes amazing how we can even justify this pre-occupation with others as a religious or spiritual concern. I know a woman who finds out some juicy bit of gossip on someone and carries it into practically every conversation she enters. Before laying out all the ugly details of hearsay gossip, she announces that she is only sharing this because "the Lord has laid it upon her heart and she is prayerfully concerned about the person." Having given herself reli-gious justification for the slander, she comfortably proceeds to blast the character of another. She has no qualms about calling her critical preoccupation with this person's prob-lems her "concerned heart." She seems completely unaware that underlying her "prayer concerns" for others is a hostile, judgmental need to defame character.

A lifestyle of responding is based on the spiritual disci-pline of minding our own business. While responding is concerned with others, it is quite clear about what it can and cannot control. It has no need to run anyone else's life. It knows quite well that running our own lives is a full-time job, and it wants others to also experience that freedom.

Another important characteristic of responding is help-ing to ease others by creating a space for them to be them-selves. Most of us can quickly name the people to whom we turn when something is troubling us. Almost without excep-tion, such people tend to be relaxed, nonjudgmental, and comfortable to be around. We can breathe easily around them. We can allow our thoughts and feelings to unfold. We don't have to censor ourselves. In short, we feel nonthreatened enough to explore what is bothering us.

I have read no more beautiful description of this process than Henri Nouwen's definition of the word "hospitality." Nouwen believes that the term has a very rich meaning, part of which has been lost and in need of being restored.

> Hospitality, therefore, means primarily the creation of a free space where the stranger can enter and become a friend instead of an enemy. Hospitality is not to change people, but to offer them space where change can take place. It is not to bring men and women over to our side, but to offer freedom not disturbed by dividing lines. It is not to lead our neighbor into a corner where there are no alternatives left, but to open a wide spectrum of options for choice and commitment....The paradox of hospitality is that it wants to create emptiness, not a fearful emptiness, but a friendly emptiness where strangers can enter and discover themselves as created free; free to sing their own songs, speak their own languages, dance their own dances; free also to leave and follow their own vocations. Hospitality is not a subtle invitation to adopt the lifestyle of the host, but the gift of a chance for the guest to find his own.[13]

It is not an accident that many social outcasts felt "at home" with Jesus. Prostitutes didn't *feel* like prostitutes and thieves didn't *feel* like thieves. Instead, they felt like much more. They began to feel the dignity of being God's creation. The capacity of love to move into the shadows and care for the person permitted the beginnings of freedom.

Another habit that will help in our ability to respond rather than react is to seek positive activities and thoughts rather than opportunities to judge. At a workshop I once attended, I remember hearing Wayne Muller, minister and psychotherapist, describe how a stampeding elephant can nearly tear up a village, *until* he is given something to hold onto with his long trunk.[14] Similarly, he said, our minds need something hopeful and positive to hold. Otherwise, we can be quite capable of negative, even destructive, thinking. When our minds are not seeking truth, beauty, goodness, and other healthy things, we are often vulnerable to a "take-over" by judgmental, poisonous thinking.

Another way of putting this is simply to say that a positive mind does not have the time or energy to waste on useless judgmentalism. It is too busy following a healthy path to get bogged down in a pessimistic world. A desire for expansion, growth, and improvement is much more important. Our ambition prevents us from a need to put down others.

When our judgmental tendencies are the most active, it is normally because our minds are inactive, bored, and uninterested in our own spiritual and emotional growth. During this void, blasting others can become our hobby. When we cease to talk about ideas, refuse to discuss how we are feeling, and lose sight of the hurts and struggles of those around us, we may very well engage in character attacks. After all, they make for an easy, relatively effortless, conversation.

Another ingredient in a responding mentality is the deliberate practice of empathy. The ability to understand the feelings of another is a skill we can practice. Again, many think of empathy as requiring us to feel the exact feelings someone else feels. Actually, however, that can block the process of empathy. The key is to *understand* another's feelings rather than to feel them yourself. That understanding may, of course, trigger some of our own feelings, but the

point is to place ourselves in another's shoes and take on his or her perspective. As we have already noted, this does not mean that we always agree with them. But we can make enormous progress in seeing why they think and feel the way they do.

This point needs to be heavily stressed because a lot of us may think that we are not very emotional people, and hence, not very good at empathizing with anyone. We may even think that empathy is simply a skill some are born with and others are not. The fact is, however, that empathy can be learned and taught. We may not feel like a "natural" in the empathy business, but we *can* make definite progress in improving our ability to take on another's perspective.

It helps when we daily commit ourselves to understanding *people* before criticizing *behavior*. We remind ourselves that all behavior occurs in a context, and if we have no knowledge of the context, it's probably wise to withhold judgment. We need to remember how much we dislike being judged by someone who doesn't know *our* situation. Here is a perfect opportunity to treat others as we wish to be treated. This is an opportunity to recognize our common humanity with others and not pretend that their wrongful actions are totally foreign to us. I especially appreciate the words of Bill W. of Alcoholics Anonymous:

> Finally, we begin to see that all people, including ourselves, are to some extent emotionally ill as well as frequently wrong, and then we approach true tolerance and see what real love for our fellows actually means. It will become more and more evident as we go forward that it is pointless to become angry, or to get hurt by people who, like us, are suffering from the pains of growing up.[15]

Another key to responding is embracing our emotions and our behavior as *our* responsibility. By contrast, the underlying belief in a reacting mentality is that someone else causes us to feel and think the way we do. They push our buttons and we cannot help ourselves.

I remember once talking with a sixth grader who had gotten in trouble in his class. He was standing in the hallway with a sense of confusion on his face. I was in his school that day because I was to give a guest presentation on mental health issues. I asked him how things were going. He immediately told me that he had done nothing wrong and shouldn't have to be in the hall. He said that a boy had called him a name and so he hit him. He said, "The kid called me a name, made fun of me, so what did the teacher expect?" What was crystal clear as we talked was that he fully believed that the name he had been called *forced* him in to hitting his classmate. He had no other choice. The words of another instantly provoked his arm to raise and the strike to occur. It was cut-and-dried.

What this likable boy did not realize, of course, is that being verbally put down does not necessitate hitting someone. He believed he *had* to react. He had no choice of whether to hit or not to hit the kid, so he should not be held responsible. The other boy "made" him strike out.

Unfortunately, many of us do not develop beyond this type of cause/effect thinking. Outsiders "make" us upset, "cause" us to be angry, "hurt" our feelings, or "drive" us crazy. By not owning our feelings as our responsibility, we reinforce the belief that external factors control our inner life. When we look at the Gospels, we find that no one "made" Jesus do anything. His response came from his own centeredness in the will of God.

A responding mentality, therefore, nurtures a sense of choice. We can learn to pause between someone's action and our response. We can choose from within ourselves how we want to handle the situation. Karen Horney used to talk about this as making sure our "center of gravity" is within ourselves and not in other people.[16] Our response is initiated from within. This is freedom at its best.

Viktor Frankl's inspiring words, describing his experience in a concentration camp, illustrate this point so well:

> We who lived in concentration camps can remember the men who walked through the huts comforting others, giving away their last piece of bread. They may have been few in number, but they offer sufficient proof that everything can be taken from a man but one thing: the last of the human freedoms—to choose one's attitude in any given set of circumstances, to choose one's own way....In the final analysis it becomes clear that the sort of person the prisoner became was the result of an inner decision, and not the result of camp influences alone. Fundamentally, therefore, any man can, even under such circumstances, decide what shall become of him—mentally and spiritually. He may retain his human dignity even in a concentration camp.[17]

A responding mentality also generates an awareness of our own shortcomings. This is not a debilitating, shaming awareness of our own dark side, but a keen perception of our human limitations. We see a clear link with other people's weakness because we are quite aware of our own. Others' mistakes don't seem so foreign or unusual to us.

When we react to another, on the other hand, it is often because we are actually fighting something within ourselves. Unaware of our own issues, we attempt to defeat our anxiety by attacking these same problems in others. As we become more friendly with our own dark side, we have less need to assault others. Or as I have put it in a previous book, when we accept our own "troll," it is amazing how much more accepting we are of others.[18]

Another characteristic of a responding mentality is ignoring spicy, hearsay gossip. There will probably always be a curiosity when we hear gossip (particularly controversial gossip), yet a responding mentality does not take it seriously and certainly does not obsess about it. It sees gossip as gossip, not necessarily as reality. Our minds are too busy with other matters to wallow in the tales of someone else's follies or woes. Again, it's not that we have no interest at all; it's just that our interest is a reserved, calm recognition of how imagination can push things far out of proportion.

Many, of course, thrive on gossip. In fact, it is practically the only thing they want to discuss. They are perpetually "shocked," "outraged," "flabbergasted" or "delighted" at what they hear about another. Checking out reality becomes irrelevant. They've heard it, so it must be true. Scores of examples could be cited to illustrate how untrue gossip can destroy someone's good name.

An important quality of a responding attitude is that it nourishes grace for ourselves and others. With gentleness and care, our actions and behavior stem from our own "centeredness." Our primary disposition toward ourselves and others is one of openness and not condemnation. We *practice* grace. We see the pointlessness of sarcasm; the futile consequences of self-condemnation; and the poison of putting down others. We follow the "en-couraging" life of Jesus, embracing the people underneath their dysfunctional behavior.

And finally, a responding mentality simply gives others

the benefit of the doubt. With a generous heart, it is not quick to assume that someone is guilty unless there is clear and uncontestable evidence. It is more interested in encouraging the positives in another than "catching" the negatives. While we are aware of the dangers and problems in the world, we also see the potential for wholeness.

In Summary

The most powerful, transforming gift we can offer one another is the gift of acceptance. Acceptance helps motivate people by allowing their fear and defenses to fade so that change can happen. It is the central theme of the gospel, the very backbone of psychotherapy, the most important factor in support groups (all the way from A.A. to Parent Effectiveness), the crucial ingredient in friendship, and the key to family relationships. Our greatest opportunity is to nurture and cultivate God's acceptance within ourselves and extend that grace outward to those around us.

Notes

1. Quoted in Elizabeth O'Connor, *Our Many Selves*. New York: Harper & Row, 1971, pp. 88-89.

2. Viktor Frankl, *The Will to Meaning*. New York: New American Library, 1969, p. 8.

3. Quoted in Leslie Weatherhead, *The Christian Agnostic*. Nashville: Abingdon, 1965, p. 274.

4. Harold Kushner, *When Bad Things Happen to Good People*. New York: Avon Books, 1981, pp. 88-90.

5. Leslie Weatherhead, op. cit., p. 277.

6. Harold Kushner, op. cit.

7. I have been heavily influenced on this issue by the writings of Peter Berger. See, especially, *The Sacred Canopy*. New York: Doubleday, 1967; *The Heretical Imperative*. New York: Doubleday, 1979.

8. Robert Gould, *Transformations*. New York: Simon and Schuster, 1978, p. 100.

9. Karen Horney, *Neurosis and Human Growth*. New York: W.W. Norton, 1950.

10. Ibid., p. 159.

11. Peter Berger, *The Heretical Imperative*, op. cit., p. 198.

12. Blaise Pascal, *Pensées*. New York: Modern Library, 1941, p. 25.

13. Henri Nouwen, *Reaching Out*. New York: Image Books, 1975, pp. 71-72.

14. This workshop was held at "Spirit Lodge" in Kansas City, Mo. I thoroughly recommend Wayne Muller's fine book, *The Legacy of the Heart: The Spiritual Advantages of a Painful Childhood*. New York: Simon and Schuster, 1992.

15. Alcoholics Anonymous, *Twelve Steps and Twelve Traditions*. New York: Alcoholics World Services, 1951, p. 92.

16. Karen Horney, op. cit.

17. Viktor Frankl, *Man's Search for Meaning*. New York: Washington Square Press, 1963, pp. 104-5.

18. Terry D. Cooper, *Accepting the Troll Underneath the Bridge*. Mahwah, N.J.: Paulist Press, 1996.